FIGHTING IN FLANDERS
GAS. MUD. MEMORY.

MÉLANIE MORIN-PELLETIER

CANADIAN WAR MUSEUM
MUSÉE CANADIEN DE LA GUERRE

Library and Archives Canada
Cataloguing in Publication

Morin-Pelletier, Mélanie
Fighting in Flanders – gas, mud, memory /
Mélanie Morin-Pelletier.

(Souvenir catalogue series, 2291-6385)
Issued also in French under title: Se battre en Flandre –
gaz, boue, mémoire.
Includes bibliographical references.
ISBN 978-0-660-20306-5
Cat. no.: NM23-5/8-2014E

1. World War, 1914-1918 – Campaigns – Belgium – Exhibitions.
2. Canada. Canadian Army – History – World War, 1914-1918 – Exhibitions.
3. Canada. Canadian Army. Canadian Expeditionary Force – History – Exhibitions.
4. World War, 1914-1918 – Canada – Exhibitions.
5. World War, 1914-1918 – Campaigns – Belgium – Flanders – Exhibitions.
6. Canadian War Museum – Exhibitions.

I. Canadian War Museum.
II. Title.
III. Series: Souvenir catalogue series.

D542 Y5 M67 2014
940.4'144
C2014-980041-X

Published by the
Canadian War Museum
1 Vimy Place
Ottawa, ON K1A 0M8
www.warmuseum.ca

Printed and bound in Canada.

This work is a souvenir of the exhibition **Fighting in Flanders**, which was developed by the Canadian War Museum in partnership with the Memorial Museum Passchendaele 1917, Belgium, and with the generous support of the E. W. Bickle Foundation.

Souvenir Catalogue series, 8
ISSN 2291-6385

VISIT**FLANDERS**

Over the period of four long years, Flanders Fields was the dramatic scene of some of the bloodiest battles of the First World War. Starting in 1914, the peaceful landscape was transformed into a battlefield. The war did not only affect Europeans; people from all over the world, especially from Canada, came to fight in Flanders. A million soldiers were wounded, killed, or missing in action. Thousands of citizens lost their homes and became refugees. The war devastated entire cities and villages — destroyed them beyond recognition.

Today, the landscape of the region still tells the story of the war. There are hundreds of monuments and cemeteries that are of great historical significance to people from all over the world. Visitors can explore a variety of interactive museums in the area, each bringing different aspects of the conflict to life.

Ceremonies like the Last Post show that the fallen are never forgotten. From 2014 to 2018, Flanders will commemorate the hundredth anniversary of the Great War. The Flemish Government has set up an ambitious four-year remembrance project, known as the Great War Centenary, to commemorate the victims of the war and to reflect on peace and understanding.

By sponsoring **Fighting in Flanders**, VISIT**FLANDERS** would like to honour Canada's incredible support of our region. We hope this exhibition and catalogue will inspire you to visit Flanders Fields and to experience our history and culture.

Flanders
State of the Art

IN FLANDERS FIELDS

In Flanders fields the poppies blow
Between the crosses, row on row,
That mark our place; and in the sky
The larks, still bravely singing, fly
Scarce heard amid the guns below.

We are the Dead. Short days ago
We lived, felt dawn, saw sunset glow,
Loved, and were loved, and now we lie
In Flanders fields.

Take up our quarrel with the foe:
To you from failing hands we throw
The torch; be yours to hold it high.
If ye break faith with us who die
We shall not sleep, though poppies grow
In Flanders fields.

— **John McCrae**

CONTENTS

FOREWORD

From my office in the Canadian War Museum, it's a brisk 15-minute walk to the National War Monument in downtown Ottawa, where the Tomb of the Unknown Soldier lies.

The man whose remains rest in the tomb was one of more than 61,000 Canadian soldiers who died during the First World War. In those battlefields, churned by artillery and subsumed in mud, thousands perished without leaving a trace of their identity. Many were buried in unmarked graves; some still lie beneath the farmers' fields in France and Belgium where war once raged. Countless Canadian soldiers have lost their lives in past conflicts. The Unknown Soldier represents them all.

Every year on November 11, thousands of Canadians gather in the square around the National War Monument, to mark the anniversary of the end of the First World War. Pinned to the coats and sweaters that muffle the multitude against the chilly fall air, are thousands of bright red poppies — flowers that have come to symbolize remembrance, thanks to Lieutenant-Colonel John McCrae's famous First World War poem, *In Flanders Fields*. The poppies, and the Tomb of the Unknown Soldier, remind us of the sacrifices and contributions that Canadians made during the First World War.

The exhibition **Fighting in Flanders — Gas. Mud. Memory.** focusses on the portion of the war fought in Belgium by Canadian troops. This region saw some of the conflict's most deadly and horrifying battles, whose names remain engraved on the Canadian psyche even today: the Second Battle of Ypres, where 6,000 Canadians were killed or injured in the Germans' first deployment of chlorine gas; the Battle of Mount Sorrel, where, despite 8,700 casualties, Canadians recaptured lost ground with massive firepower; and the Battle of Passchendaele, where a sea of mud made Canadian soldiers easy targets for enemy guns, and victory came at the cost of nearly 16,000 Canadian casualties.

Beyond the battles, **Fighting in Flanders — Gas. Mud. Memory.** explores the technologies and strategies, developed by Canadians and their allies, which allowed combat troops to adapt to the terrible conditions in the field. Further, it describes the memorials erected after the war and the gestures of remembrance that continue today.

This exhibition would not have been possible without the generous support of our sponsors and the many national and international partners whose artifacts, documents, and artworks appear in this exhibition alongside material from the Museum's own extensive collection. These objects provide a touchstone for people today to remember the experiences — personal, national, and international — of the generation who fought the First World War.

James Whitham

Director General,
Canadian War Museum,
and Vice-President,
Canadian Museum of History

INTRODUCTION

Belgium was an integral part of Canadians' experience of the First World War. The German Empire's invasion of Belgium was the reason Canada, as a member of the British Empire, entered the war on August 4, 1914. Moreover, Canada's war began and ended in Belgium: the fledgling Canadian Expeditionary Force experienced its first major action at Ypres in April 1915, and Canadian soldiers marched into Mons at the end of the war in November 1918. Canada also won significant victories on Belgian soil. These victories included defeating German attacks at the Second Battle of Ypres in 1915 and the Battle of Mount Sorrel in 1916, as well as capturing Passchendaele ridge in 1917.

Soldiers fighting in the First World War faced unprecedented challenges. The world's first industrial-scale conflict led to the mass-production of terrible weapons, including poisonous gas, massed artillery and machine guns. The war laid waste the Belgian countryside, leaving it criss-crossed with hundreds of kilometres of barbed wire and trenches, and pockmarked with thousands of shell craters. Although success often came at considerable cost, the military achievements made by Canadian troops in Belgium can be attributed in part to their ability to adapt to and overcome this demanding environment.

Destruction at Ypres, Belgium

One hundred years later, the experience of Canadian soldiers in Belgium is still reflected in the way Canada remembers and commemorates the First World War and other conflicts. *In Flanders Fields*, perhaps the most famous poem of the First World War, was written by Lieutenant-Colonel John McCrae in the immediate aftermath of the Second Battle of Ypres, where McCrae had lost a close friend. The poem was immediately popular and remains so today. Commonly read during memorial services, *In Flanders Fields* also inspired the use of the poppy as a symbol of remembrance around the world.

This souvenir catalogue is a companion to **Fighting in Flanders — Gas. Mud. Memory.,** an exhibition that explores how Canadians experienced, adapted to and later remembered the First World War in Belgium. Created by the Canadian War Museum, the exhibition features artifacts, art and archival material from the Museum's extensive collection, as well as material contributed by a number of national and international partners. Ranging from small poppy lapel pins to a 7,000-kilogram artillery piece, the artifacts in the exhibition present a powerful record of Canada's war in Belgium between 1915 and 1918. The exhibition and this companion publication encourage Canadians to reflect on the personal, national and international reach of the First World War.

THE BRITISH EMPIRE AT WAR

The British Empire went to war when Germany refused to respect Belgium's neutrality and invaded the country.

The Belgian invasion was part of Germany's strategy to advance through Western Europe. It violated an agreement signed in 1839 between Great Britain, Germany, France, Russia and Austria-Hungary, and led to Great Britain declaring war on the pretext of defending Belgium's neutrality. In 1914, German Chancellor Theobald von Bethmann Hollweg caused worldwide outrage when he dismissed the 1839 Treaty of London as a mere "scrap of paper."

CANADA'S WAR IN BELGIUM

Canadians who fought in Belgium during the First World War adapted to horrific battlefield conditions with grim determination.

Canadian soldiers faced poison gas during the Second Battle of Ypres, used massive firepower to recapture lost ground at Mount Sorrel and made their way through a sea of mud to seize the village of Passchendaele. To this day, their contribution to the defence of Belgium is remembered and actively commemorated.

The "Scrap of Paper"
Recruitment Poster

June 1915

Fugitives at Sea

Between 1914 and 1919
Gerald Spencer Pryse (1882-1956)

WITNESS

Major Gerald Spencer Pryse, a Welsh artist who served as a despatch rider for the Belgian government during the war, saw Belgian refugees displaced as a result of the German invasion. His sketches of these scenes were used to create many recruitment and fundraising posters.

A SYMBOL OF DESTRUCTION

A few kilometres behind the front lines stood the shattered city of Ypres, Belgium. At the heart of the city was the 500-year-old Cloth Hall, illustrated on the following page. One of the largest commercial buildings of the Middle Ages, it was a legacy of the city's textile industry.

Damaged by artillery shells in early November 1914, then nearly destroyed by incendiary shells two weeks later, the Cloth Hall became an important symbol of the massive destruction brought by the conflict. For decades after the war, it was meticulously reconstructed to its original medieval designs.

Cloth Hall, Ypres, 1914

Alfred Bastien (1873–1955)

UNITED KINGDOM

NETHERLANDS

GERMAN EMPIRE

Western Front
Ypres
St. Eloi
Passchendaele
Mt. Sorrel
Festubert
Lens
Vimy
Arras
Cambrai
Beaumont-Hamel
Courcelette
Amiens

Brussels

BELGIUM

Mons

FRANCE

LUXEM-BOURG

Yser

Lys

Meuse

Somme

0   100   200 km

Belgium and the Western Front

Late 1914

Protecting Soldiers and Animals Against Gas

GAS

THE SECOND BATTLE OF YPRES

1915

At the Second Battle of Ypres, in April 1915, Canadian and Allied soldiers fought through lethal chlorine gas to hold the city of Ypres.

"It is impossible for me to give a real idea of the terror and horror spread among us all by this filthy loathsome pestilence."

— **Major Harold Matthews**, 8th Battalion

"The effects of this gas are pitiful to see, a great many of the victims passed us on their way back for treatment. They are practically blind and nearly smothered."

— **Lieutenant Edmund MacNachtan**, 1st Brigade, Canadian Field Artillery

Gas Attack on the Somme Using Gas Canisters

THE BATTLE

April 22 to 24, 1915

The Germans released 160 tons of chlorine gas from 5,730 cylinders. It formed a massive greenish-yellow cloud, which hit the French first. They ran away from the gas, coughing, choking and dying.

The French collapse created a six-kilometre breach in the Allied line. Canadian reserves were rushed to the front to cover the gap in order to stop the German advance. The Canadians attacked aggressively, forcing the enemy back along the front and preventing a breakthrough.

In the days that followed the initial attack, the Allies succeeded in fighting the Germans to a standstill. But the progress took its toll: over the four-day battle, Canadian soldiers suffered approximately 6,000 casualties.

A GLIMPSE INTO BATTLE

Army regulations prohibited soldiers from taking pictures with their own cameras for fear that they could fall into the hands of the enemy and be used to German advantage. Nevertheless, many soldiers defied the rules. A hundred years later, these photographs provide an unofficial record of the Second Battle of Ypres.

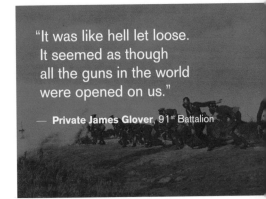

"It was like hell let loose. It seemed as though all the guns in the world were opened on us."

— **Private James Glover**, 91st Battalion

Two Soldiers in Shallow Trench

Ypres
1915

7 A.M., April 22nd, 1915

Arthur Nantel (1874-1948)

CAPTAIN FRANCIS SCRIMGER, V.C.

Captain Francis Scrimger, a physician from Montréal, Quebec, commanded a medical station at Wieltje, 5 kilometres northeast of Ypres. Scrimger was one of the first to identify the gas as chlorine. He instructed Canadian soldiers to hold a damp cloth over the mouth and nose to protect the lungs. While not entirely effective, this provided some protection, allowing the soldiers to continue fighting.

Captain Francis Scrimger earned the Victoria Cross for his bravery and devotion to his patients on April 25, 1915.

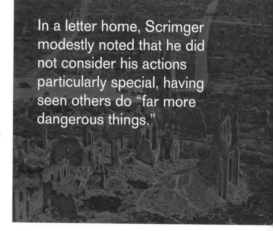

In a letter home, Scrimger modestly noted that he did not consider his actions particularly special, having seen others do "far more dangerous things."

***Portrait of
Captain F. A. C.
Scrimger,
Victoria Cross***

Between 1915 and 1918
Archibald George Barnes
(1887-1972)

**Victoria Cross Medal Set,
Captain Francis Scrimger, V.C.**

DELIVERING GAS

At Ypres in 1915, chlorine gas was transported to the front as a liquid in cylinders. Chlorine cooled to its gaseous form when exposed to the air and the wind then carried it to enemy lines. This dependence on weather conditions meant that some attacks had to be delayed.

The introduction of chemical bombs was an improvement over gas cylinders because a favourable wind was no longer necessary. In addition, it increased the effective range of gas.

Livens Projector Gas Bomb

PROTECTIVE EQUIPMENT

After the initial use of chlorine gas during the Second Battle of Ypres, Allied commanders recognized the urgent need to devise defensive gas equipment to better protect soldiers in the trenches.

When developing gas masks, a number of factors had to be balanced, including effectiveness of protection, comfort and ease of use. Some masks were better than others, but none of them met all of the soldiers' requirements.

Issued to Canadian soldiers in May 1915, the Black Veil respirator consisted of a gauze pad soaked in chemicals to guard against chlorine gas. Although it provided adequate protection when worn properly, the mask had a tendency to shift as soldiers moved in battle, rendering it ineffective.

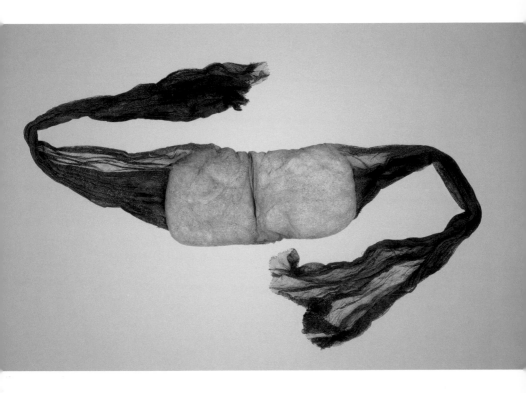

Black Veil Respirator

HYPO HELMET

The Hypo helmet was a chemically treated bag that offered protection against chlorine gas. It was developed in the summer of 1915 by Captain Cluny Macpherson, a medical officer from Newfoundland.

Worn over the head and tucked in at the neck, it was less prone to displacement than the Black Veil respirator. However, it was cumbersome and stifling, and the bag's chemical treatment irritated the skin and eyes.

P.H. HELMET

The P.H. (phenate hexamine) helmet replaced the Hypo helmet in the fall of 1915. It featured a valve through which the soldier exhaled, preventing a build-up of carbon dioxide inside the helmet.

The P.H. helmet provided adequate protection against chlorine gas and phosgene. It was, however, unpopular with soldiers because they did not like having to tuck it carefully into their shirts and the helmet's chemical treatment often burned their skin.

Hypo Helmet

**Canadian Soldier
Wearing a P.H. Helmet**

SMALL BOX RESPIRATOR

Introduced in August 1916, the Small Box Respirator remained the best respirator used by the British and the Canadians for the duration of the war. With a filter to keep out irritants and a face mask available in four sizes, it offered adequate protection, reasonable comfort, and ease of use.

GAS ALARM

Without adequate warning, soldiers were unable to don their gas masks in time to prevent breathing in the toxic chemicals. Soldiers on sentry duty were expected to watch for signs of poison gas. By sounding the alarm at the first hint of gas, they let their comrades know that they should quickly put on their masks to avoid death or injury.

A soldier's keen sense of smell could save his life. The sooner he detected the odor of poison gas and put on his protective gear, the greater his chances of survival.

Small Box Respirator

**Canadian Soldier Wearing
a Small Box Respirator**

Gas Chamber at Seaford

1918
Frederick Varley (1881-1969)

GAS-TESTING EXERCISES

This painting by Frederick Varley depicts a gas-training exercise in Seaford, England, simulating battlefield conditions. Soldiers are shown emerging from a gas-filled hut that they had to pass through. Using protective equipment, the training helped build confidence.

Anti-gas protection and training were critical, as there was very little that doctors and nurses could do to relieve the suffering of gassed patients.

EQUIPMENT-TESTING STATIONS

Signs were posted near gas-testing stations on the field. Soldiers were instructed to enter the facilities to have their equipment tested.

Gas Alarm

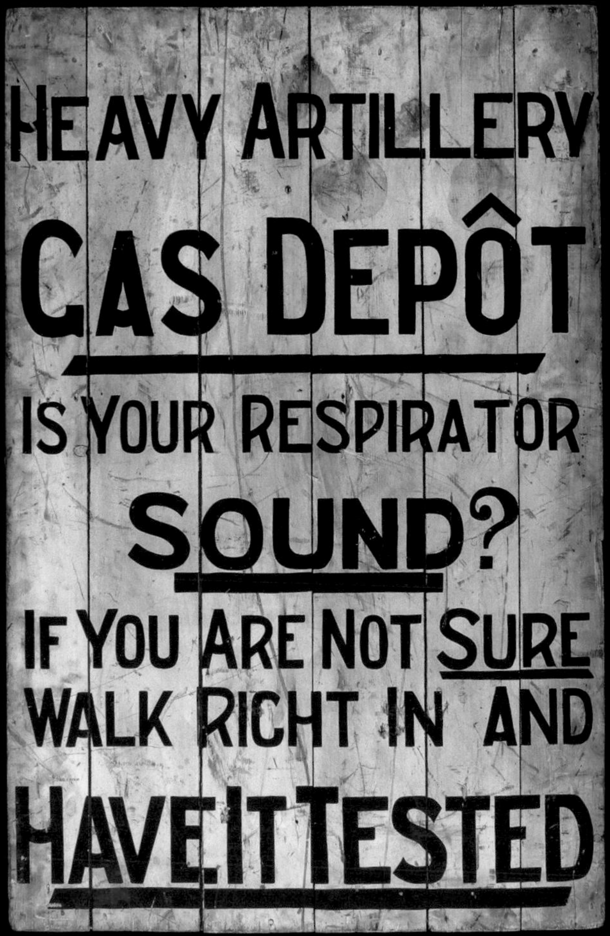

HEAVY ARTILLERY
CAS DEPÔT
IS YOUR RESPIRATOR
SOUND?
IF YOU ARE NOT SURE
WALK RIGHT IN AND
HAVE IT TESTED

This sign instructs soldiers to enter a gas respirator testing station to make sure that their protective equipment is working properly.

Heavy Howitzer in Action

1916

FIREPOWER

THE BATTLE OF MOUNT SORREL

1916

The Canadians lost the first phase of the Battle of Mount Sorrel. With careful preparation and massive firepower, they were able to recapture the ground.

"Now when we came out you would have swore that we had been in a slaughter house. Our clothes were completely saturated and stiff with blood and guts."

— **Private Stanley Russell Bowe**,
2nd Canadian Mounted Rifles

Devastated Landscape

Sanctuary Wood
1916

THE BATTLE

June 2 to 14, 1916

On June 2, 1916, the Germans launched an intensive bombardment on Canadian positions at Mount Sorrel. They intended to seize the last remaining high ground in the Ypres region still in Allied hands. The attack devastated the Canadians, who suffered heavy losses and had to retreat from several of their positions.

To recapture Mount Sorrel, British and Canadian leaders planned to destroy enemy lines with massed artillery fire and then launch an infantry attack to retake the ground. To carry out this plan, they assembled 218 guns to fire on a front of about 1,500 metres. It was an impressive array of firepower for such a narrow front. The successful operation came with a heavy price: over 8,700 Canadian soldiers were killed or wounded.

This counterattack featured elements that would characterize the Canadian approach to battle for years to come: careful preparation and using more firepower, instead of more soldiers, to take an objective.

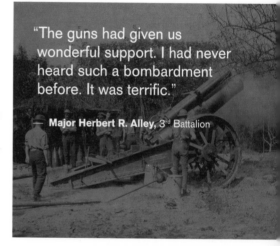

"The guns had given us wonderful support. I had never heard such a bombardment before. It was terrific."

— **Major Herbert R. Alley,** 3rd Battalion

"A Present from Canada"

DEVASTATING LOSS

At Sanctuary Wood, during the Battle of Mount Sorrel, soldiers of the Princess Patricia's Canadian Light Infantry were trapped by enemy fire. Over 400 of the battalion's 700 fighting men became casualties, including 150 who were killed. This painting by soldier-artist Kenneth Forbes depicts survivors holding the destroyed ground.

The Defence of Sanctuary Wood

1918
Kenneth Keith Forbes (1892-1980)

EVOLVING WEAPONRY — REPLACING THE ROSS RIFLE

Soldiers in the Canadian Expeditionary Force were first equipped with the Canadian-made Ross rifle. It was an excellent sniper rifle but had a tendency to jam in battle. By September 1916, Canadian divisions had replaced their Ross rifles with British Lee-Enfield rifles.

Lee-Enfield rifles were modified in military workshops during the war to serve as grenade launchers. The barrel and forestock were reinforced to withstand the force generated when firing. Using the modified Lee-Enfield rifle, soldiers could launch grenades up to 275 metres, much farther than they did by hand.

Ross Rifle
(Top)

Lee-Enfield SMLE Mk. III
(Bottom)

MACHINE GUNS

Firing several hundred bullets per minute, machine guns were especially devastating when used against enemy troops advancing over open ground. They laid down nearly continuous fire, while soldiers advanced to engage enemy strongpoints with rifles and grenades.

THE VICKERS

The Vickers machine gun was capable of sustained and accurate fire of up to 500 bullets per minute in almost any conditions. It had a well-deserved reputation for being a robust and reliable weapon that was simple to use and easy to repair.

THE LEWIS

Used by the British and Canadian forces starting in the summer of 1915, the Lewis fired up to 600 bullets per minute. It weighed 13 kilograms, about half the weight of the Vickers, and could be carried and used by a single soldier.

Vickers Mk. I Water-Cooled
(Top)

Lewis Model 1914
(Bottom)

ARTILLERY: THE STEEL DELUGE

Artillery inflicted the majority of battlefield casualties during the First World War.

The use of artillery evolved significantly. In the early years of the war, most artillery was limited to direct fire, shooting at targets in its line of sight. However, by the end of the war, artillery was capable of indirect fire, hitting targets hidden by terrain or too far away to see.

Canadians faced heavy howitzers, like the one seen here, at the Battle of Mount Sorrel. The 21 cm Mörser 10 was the standard heavy howitzer used by the Germans in the first two years of the war. It could destroy trenches up to 8,200 metres away.

**Howitzer, 21cm Mörser 10,
Rifled Breech Loading**

**The German Mörser
in Action**

AIR AND GROUND COOPERATION

Pilots and gunners learned to cooperate during the First World War.

On June 7 and 8, 1916, pilots took aerial photographs of Mount Sorrel by flying dangerously slow and low over the German positions. Gunners used the photographs to target enemy strongpoints. For the Canadians, this marked the beginning of interaction between artillery and aircraft.

AERIAL PHOTOGRAPHY

This collage shows aerial photographs taken of the region around Mount Sorrel in July 1916. On the left, the photographs are arranged to show how they were used to create maps.

**Aerial
Photograph of
the Ypres Salient**

July 1916

Ypres Salient, July 1916.

Hooge—Armagh Wood.

"Mud and water through which the Canadians had to advance to Passchendaele. The water in places was 10 feet deep."

MUD

THE BATTLE OF PASSCHENDAELE

1917

The Battle of Passchendaele took place between July 31 and November 10, 1917. Canadian soldiers joined the fight in October, overcoming a sea of mud to capture Passchendaele.

"The mud is our worst enemy. You could hardly imagine how bad it is."

— **Private Harold Henry Simpson**, 2nd Canadian Siege Battery

THE BATTLE

July 31 to November 10, 1917

British Commander-in-Chief Sir Douglas Haig launched an offensive to seize the highlands of Passchendaele Ridge and, from there, capture the German-occupied channel ports.

After some initial success, the British offensive ground to a halt. In August, unexpectedly heavy rains turned the soil into a sea of mud. Haig sanctioned an attack to take Passchendaele on October 12, 1917, but atrocious battlefield conditions prevented the British from taking the ridge.

"We were soaked through with rain and perspiration from the efforts we had been making to get through the clinging mud."

— **Private John Pritchard Sudbury**, 73rd Battalion

British Commander-in-Chief Sir Douglas Haig (right)
with Lieutenant-General Arthur Currie

1918

LIEUTENANT-GENERAL ARTHUR CURRIE'S PLAN

Passchendaele Ridge was a slope leading up to the ruined village of Passchendaele. It was divided in two by an overflowing river.

As shown on this map, Arthur Currie divided the soldiers in two columns and planned for them to attack on each side of the river. Currie believed that the only way to capture the flooded and well defended ridge was to take it one position at a time. He planned four small-scale operations, each designed to capture and hold a key position.

CANADIANS IN BATTLE

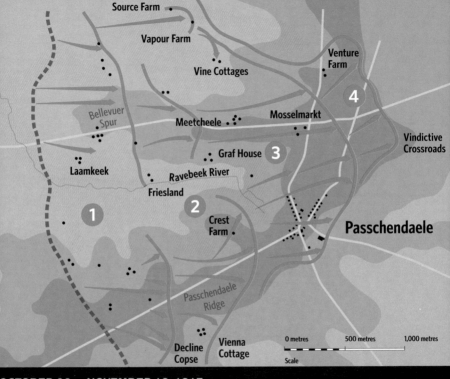

Source Farm

Vapour Farm

Vine Cottages

Venture Farm

Bellevuer Spur

Meetcheele

Mosselmarkt

Vindictive Crossroads

Graf House

3

4

Laamkeek

Ravebeek River

Friesland

2

1

Crest Farm

Passchendaele

Passchendaele Ridge

Decline Copse

Vienna Cottage

| 0 metres | 500 metres | 1,000 metres |

Scale

OCTOBER 26 – NOVEMBER 10, 1917

1 October 26-28

2 October 30

3 November 6

4 November 10

— Front Line

- - - Start Line, October 26

→ Canadian Attack

● Pillboxes, German defensive positions

■ ▬ Building

▨ Flooded Area

**Canadian Pioneers Laying
Duckboards over the Mud**

Passchendaele
1917

DUCKBOARDS

Soldiers in the First World War referred to these wooden platforms as "duckboards" or "trench mats." Kilometres of duckboards were laid over the Belgian soil by pioneer battalions, who performed construction tasks. In Passchendaele, duckboards were particularly important to help soldiers advance to the front lines and avoid drowning in mud.

"We used to walk along these wooden duckboards — like ladders laid on the ground. If a man was hit and wounded and fell off he could easily drown in the mud and never be seen again. You just did not want to go off the duckboards."

— **Private Richard Mercer**,
1st Canadian Motor Machine Gun Brigade

Duckboard

GUNNERS IN THE MUD

Gunners performed the exhausting work
of moving heavy artillery pieces into position.
They spent hours building firm wooden
platforms from which the guns could
be fired without sinking into the mud.

This painting by Belgian artist Alfred Bastien
depicts a group of Canadian gunners
at Passchendaele as they push, pull,
and lift a wagon out of the mud.

***Canadian Gunners in the Mud,
Passchendaele***

1917
Alfred Bastien (1873-1955)

GERMAN PILLBOXES

The deep mud made it very difficult to build trenches. Instead, the Germans constructed hundreds of pillboxes to protect their positions.

Pillboxes were small fortresses made of 1.5-metre-thick reinforced concrete. Their primary role was to protect troops from artillery shells. They could withstand direct hits from all but the heaviest artillery pieces.

A Flooded German Pillbox

Passchendaele
1917

VICTORIA CROSS RECIPIENTS

Capturing a pillbox was a dangerous enterprise. Five Canadians soldiers — Corporal Colin Barron, Sergeant Tommy Holmes, Lieutenant Hugh McKenzie, Sergeant George Mullin and Captain Christopher O'Kelly — played a crucial role in capturing pillboxes during the Battle of Passchendaele. For their bravery, they were awarded the Victoria Cross, the British Empire's highest award for military valour.

Corporal Colin Barron, V.C.

2005
Sharif Jean Charle Tarabay (1958-)

Sergeant T. W. Holmes, V.C.

Around 1918
Ernest George Fosbery (1874–1960)

Lieutenant Hugh McKenzie, V.C.

2005
Sharif Jean Charle Tarabay (1958–)

Portrait of Sergeant G. H. Mullin, V.C.

Around 1918
John Beatty (1869-1941)

Portrait of Captain C. P. J. O'Kelly, V.C.

1918
Frederick Varley (1881-1969)

THE WONDER WEAPON?

Tanks were developed to overcome the stalemate of trench warfare. Capable of driving over enemy trenches, the armoured vehicles also offered protection to soldiers advancing on enemy positions. At the Battle of Passchendaele, however, they sank into the mud and were left vulnerable to shelling.

British Tank Partially Submerged in Mud

Passchendaele
October 1917

Passing the Menin Gate Memorial

Ypres, Belgium
October 2013

MEMORY

One Hundred Years: Belgians and Canadians Remember

THE LIBERATION OF MONS, 1918

Just hours before the Armistice was declared, on November 11, 1918, the Canadians captured the Belgian city of Mons and were greeted enthusiastically by Belgian civilians.

The Canadian soldiers were greeted as liberators by the people of Mons, who organized ceremonies and parades to mark the end of more than four years of German occupation.

**Canadian Soldiers
Marching Through Mons**

Morning of November 11, 1918

CANADIANS IN MONS

In this painting, artist Inglis Sheldon-Williams depicts Belgian civilians and Canadian soldiers celebrating in the town square at Mons. The German body in the front is evidence of the fighting that raged in and around Mons in the days leading up to the Armistice.

The Return to Mons

1920
Inglis Sheldon-Williams (1870-1940)

BURIED IN
FLANDERS FIELDS

Over 61,000 Canadian soldiers died during the First World War, including more than 10,000 in Belgium. The dead were mourned by friends and family back in Canada, and by the men who served with them.

This Roll of Honor commemorates the members of the Zion Presbyterian Church in Hull (now Gatineau, Quebec), who served in the First World War. The list includes Lieutenant Alexis Helmer, who was killed at Ypres on May 2, 1915 at the age of 22. According to a witness, Helmer's friend Lieutenant-Colonel John McCrae began writing his iconic poem, *In Flanders Fields*, in an attempt to compose himself following the burial.

Lieutenant Alexis Helmer

1914

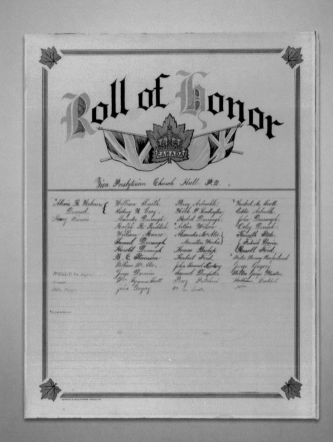

Commemorative Plaque

LIEUTENANT-COLONEL JOHN McCRAE

A native of Guelph, Ontario, and a veteran of the South African War (1899-1902), John McCrae served as a surgeon during the First World War. He was first attached to the Canadian Field Artillery and then to the No. 3 Canadian General Hospital. Frequently ill during the war, McCrae contracted pneumonia and meningitis and died on January 28, 1918. McCrae is best remembered for his poem *In Flanders Fields*.

IN FLANDERS FIELDS

In Flanders fields the poppies blow
Between the crosses, row on row,
That mark our place; and in the sky
The larks, still bravely singing, fly
Scarce heard amid the guns below.

We are the Dead. Short days ago
We lived, felt dawn, saw sunset glow,
Loved, and were loved, and now we lie
In Flanders fields.

Take up our quarrel with the foe:
To you from failing hands we throw
The torch; be yours to hold it high.
If ye break faith with us who die
We shall not sleep, though poppies grow
In Flanders fields.

John McCrae

Around 1914

In Flanders Now

1919
Edna Jaques (1891-1978)

INSPIRED BY
IN FLANDERS FIELDS

The remarkable popularity of Lieutenant-Colonel John McCrae's *In Flanders Fields* is also reflected by the many poems that were published in response to his work.

SYMBOL OF REMEMBRANCE

Deeply touched by John McCrae's poem, Moina Michael, an American who worked overseas during the war, successfully campaigned to have the American Legion recognize the poppy as an official symbol of remembrance in April 1920.

For Democracy's Fallen Defenders
Poppy Day leaflet

United States
Between 1930 and 1939

FROM EUROPE
TO NORTH AMERICA

In France, Anne Guérin vigorously advocated
the use of the poppy to commemorate
soldiers who died in the First World War.
In 1921, she travelled to Britain and Canada,
and convinced the British Legion and the
Canadian Great War Veterans Association
(a predecessor of the Royal Canadian Legion)
to adopt the poppy as their symbol
of remembrance.

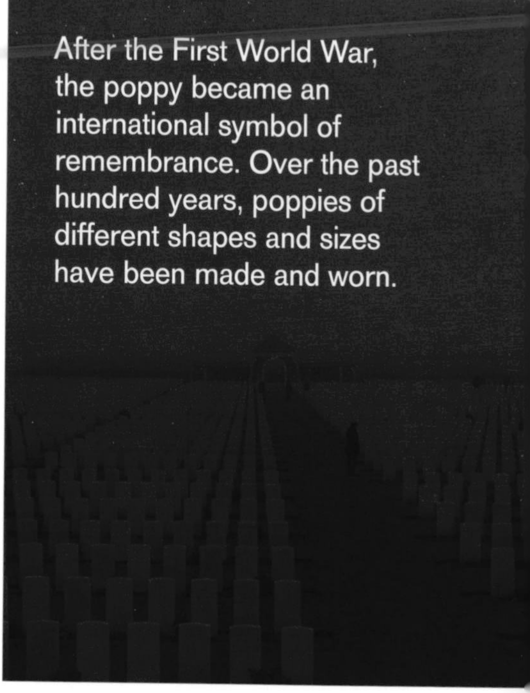

After the First World War,
the poppy became an
international symbol of
remembrance. Over the past
hundred years, poppies of
different shapes and sizes
have been made and worn.

Fabric Poppy

United Kingdom
1920s

YPRES IN PIECES

"Hosts of tourists and globe-trotters will come to see Ypres in future years, but it will never mean the same to them as to those who have seen it in its utter ruin."

— **Dr. William Boyd**, Royal Army Medical Corps

Canadian soldiers were appalled by the magnitude of the destruction they witnessed in Belgium during the war.

Collected from the ruins of the city, these two objects are physical reminders of the devastation the war brought to the entire country.

Glass Fragment

Fragment of an Angel Sculpture

The Menin Gate Memorial

Ypres, Belgium
October 2013

THE MENIN GATE MEMORIAL

Ypres is the site of the most famous Commonwealth First World War memorial, the Menin Gate Memorial. Designed by architect Reginald Blomfield, the monument was completed in 1927.

It commemorates the soldiers of the British Empire who were killed in Belgium during the First World War but have no known grave. The names of 54,404 Allied soldiers, including 6,927 Canadians, are inscribed on its walls.

LAST POST CEREMONY

Every evening, from 7:30 to 8:30, the traffic around the Menin Gate stops for the Last Post ceremony. Through this nightly tribute, the city of Ypres honours those who died defending it during the First World War.

The Last Post ceremony was introduced in 1928 and has been performed nearly 30,000 times since then. It was interrupted only when Ypres was occupied by the Germans during the Second World War, and was resumed the day after the occupation ended in September 1944.

THE BROODING SOLDIER

In 1920, a committee in Canada selected Frederick Chapman Clemesha's monument design, *The Brooding Soldier*, to serve as the central feature of the Canadian war memorial at St. Julien, Belgium.

Standing eleven metres tall, the memorial marks the ground where the 1st Canadian Division withstood a poison gas attack during the Second Battle of Ypres.

The Last Post Ceremony

Ypres, Belgium

**St. Julien
Memorial
Dedication
Ceremony**

July 8, 1923

MAKING THE MEMORIAL

Artist Frederick Chapman Clemesha is seen here with *The Brooding Soldier* under construction. In 1946, when asked why his monument was spared by the Germans during the Second World War, he replied that it was probably because of the "absence of hate" in the sculpture.

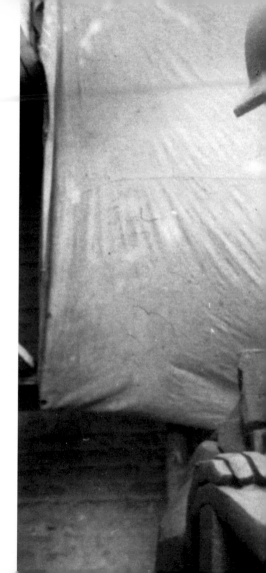

FINDING THE MISSING

A century after the outbreak of war, the remains of more than 100,000 soldiers are still missing under Belgian soil.

Several dozen bodies are retrieved every year. The police takes possession of the remains and hands them over to the war graves authorities of the appropriate country to organize formal reburial. Complex forensic work and historical research can sometimes reveal the identities of these soldiers. Seen here is a 2003 reburial of Canadian soldiers in Belgium.

THE IRON HARVEST

In 1919, the Belgian Army created a special team of soldiers to collect and dispose of hazardous materials from the former battlefields that had become farmers' fields.

In 2012, 160 tonnes of munitions were unearthed from under Ypres. It is estimated that 300 million projectiles fired during the war still lie under the soil of the Ypres region. More than 850 people have been killed or injured by these munitions since the end of the war, including 20 bomb disposal team members.

Farmers ploughing their fields have to be cautious to avoid accidentally hitting live ammunition. They gather any rusted shells and bombs that they unearth, and place them along the edges of their fields, ready for inspection, collection and disposal. This annual exercise is known as the iron harvest.

**Caporal Nico Sierens
of the Belgian Bomb Disposal Team**

2013

THE WAR IN THEIR FIELDS

Stijn Butaye grew up on Pond Farm, located 7 kilometres northeast of Ypres in St. Julien, Belgium. Pond Farm changed hands many times during the war but, in the spring of 1915, it was the headquarters of the 2nd Canadian Infantry Brigade.

The First World War is still an integral part of family life for the Butayes. Every year before plowing the fields, Stijn and his father scan the ground with metal detectors. The Butaye family has been lucky, but neighbours and friends have been wounded by explosive material.

REMEMBERING THE WAR

In 2003, Stijn started his own collection of war material unearthed in his family's farmlands. To display his findings, Stijn started a museum. He is shown here with some of the First World War objects he has discovered.

Stijn Butaye

2013

**First World War Material
Found in the Fields of Pond Farm**

CONTRIBUTIONS

I would like to thank the members of the core exhibition team: Marc Beck, Britt Braaten, Marie-Louise Deruaz, Carol Reid and Laura Brown. I have benefitted from the research assistance of Nicholas Clarke as well as the input of other colleagues at the Canadian War Museum, notably Andrew Burtch, Laura Brandon, Tim Cook and Peter MacLeod. I would like to recognize the invaluable contribution of Frédéric St-Laurent and Michel Paquette (Visou Design), of Peter Oulton (oulton + devine) and of Carla Ayukawa (Evolution Design). Thank you to the photographer Bill Kent and to Lee Wyndham (Publications Coordinator) for their help in putting together this souvenir catalogue. Finally, I would like to highlight the generous support of the individuals and organizations who have loaned objects and images that have enriched the exhibition and souvenir catalogue.

PHOTO CREDITS

© Canadian War Museum